Caryn Moya Block
Romance Cover Art
Adult Coloring Book

By

Caryn Moya Block

Copyright

ISBN-13: 978-1522748069
ISBN-10: 1522748067

Printed in the United States of America

Dedication
To my fans. You are the greatest!

About This Book:
I love to color and noticed how the adult coloring books were coming into vogue.
So I decided what better pictures to color than the beautiful covers of my books.

Alpha's Mate

Book One of the Siberian Volkov Series

A trip to Moscow brings Siberian lycanthrope, Dmitry Volkov, and his pack members out of hiding. He's looking for answers to the pack's breeding problems. But he never expected to find them in the delectable Violet Anderson. With rogue lycans causing problems in the pack, can he bring a fragile human woman home as his mate?

Wildlife photographer Violet Anderson is stopping in Moscow, before she goes on assignment to shoot the elusive Russian Gray Wolf. When she meets Dmitry at a local hotspot, the sparks fly. The animal magnetism tells her she might have just met the man of her dreams. But Violet has a couple of secrets of her own, and following a wounded animal to its lair has never been a safe thing to do.

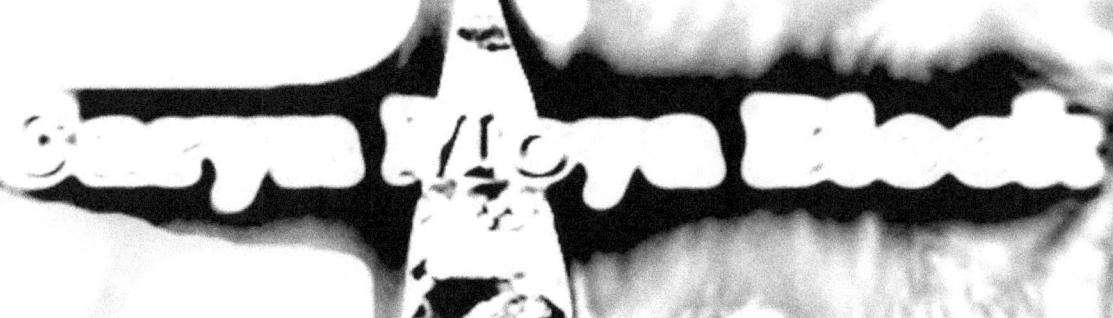

Alpha's Mate

Special Anniversary Extended Edition
Book One of the Siberian Volkov Pack Romance Series

A trip to Moscow brings Siberian lycanthrope, Dmitry Volkov, and his pack members out of hiding. He's looking for answers to the pack's breeding problems. But he never expected to find them in the delectable Violet Anderson. With rogue lycans causing problems in the pack, can he bring a fragile human woman home as his mate?

Wildlife photographer Violet Anderson is stopping in Moscow, before she goes on assignment to shoot the elusive Russian Grey Wolf. When she meets Dmitry at a local hotspot, the sparks fly. The animal magnetism tells her she might have just met the man of her dreams. But Violet has a couple of secrets of her own, and following a wounded animal to its lair has never been a safe thing to do.

Including Two Nonfiction Articles
"Why Siberia?" and "Love at First Sight, Believe in the Possibility"

ALPHA'S MATE

Special Anniversary Extended Edition
Book One of the Siberian Volkov Romance Series

Caryn Moya Block

A Siberian Werewolf in London

Book Two of the Siberian Volkov Series

Grigori Solovyov, Siberian lycanthrope, goes to London to track down a Russian mobster who is stealing from the pack. Then, Melisande Reule walks into his hotel, bringing his wolf howling to the surface. He knows he has found his mate. But when she is targeted by a Russian assassin, Grigori must fight to keep her safe and at his side.

A Siberian Werewolf In London

Caryn Moya Block

My Mate's Embrace

Book Three of the Siberian Volkov Pack Series

Anton Volkov, Siberian lycanthrope, is following the scent of Laurel Harris, who is running away from her abusive stepfather. When Anton finds her, he is surprised to realize she is his mate, the one woman meant to be his. But the Russian mafia is also on her trail. In order to rescue Laurel, Anton must first get this troubled woman to trust him. Can love heal her wounded heart?

CARYN MOYA BLOCK

MY MATE'S EMBRACE

My Magic Mate
Book Four of the Siberian Volkov Series

Brencis Solovyov, a Siberian lycanthrope, isn't looking for a mate. When he visits the local metaphysical store, he is repulsed by the owner's purple hair and combat boots. And when she gives him a potion that accidently poisons him, he fears for his life. The fact that she is his mate can only be a trick of destiny. After she claims to be a witch, he knows she is truly crazy. But there is something magical about the woman, and he isn't the only one who has noticed her strange powers. Can he keep her safe from the danger surrounding her? Will he get over his prejudice and let his magic mate cast a spell of love on him?

My Magic Mate

Caryn Moya Block

A Siberian Werewolf in Paris
Book Five of the Siberian Volkov Pack Series

Valerii Belikov, Siberian lycanthrope, knew that under the baseball cap and grubby jeans "Little Joe MacDonald" was actually Josephine. He didn't know why she was hiding, but when the mating bond snapped into place after she was injured, he never expected her to run away. Josie is his mate, the one woman meant to be his, and should have known they couldn't live apart. He could accept her hiding, but there was no way he could give her up.

Josephine Chevalier knew this day would come. Her father's killers had found her. To keep her pack mates in England safe, she needed to run. It was time to return to Paris where it all started five years ago. Now if only Valerii, the man she wanted above all others, would stay away. Looking down at the golden cord tying their hearts together, she realized he would come. How could she keep him safe?

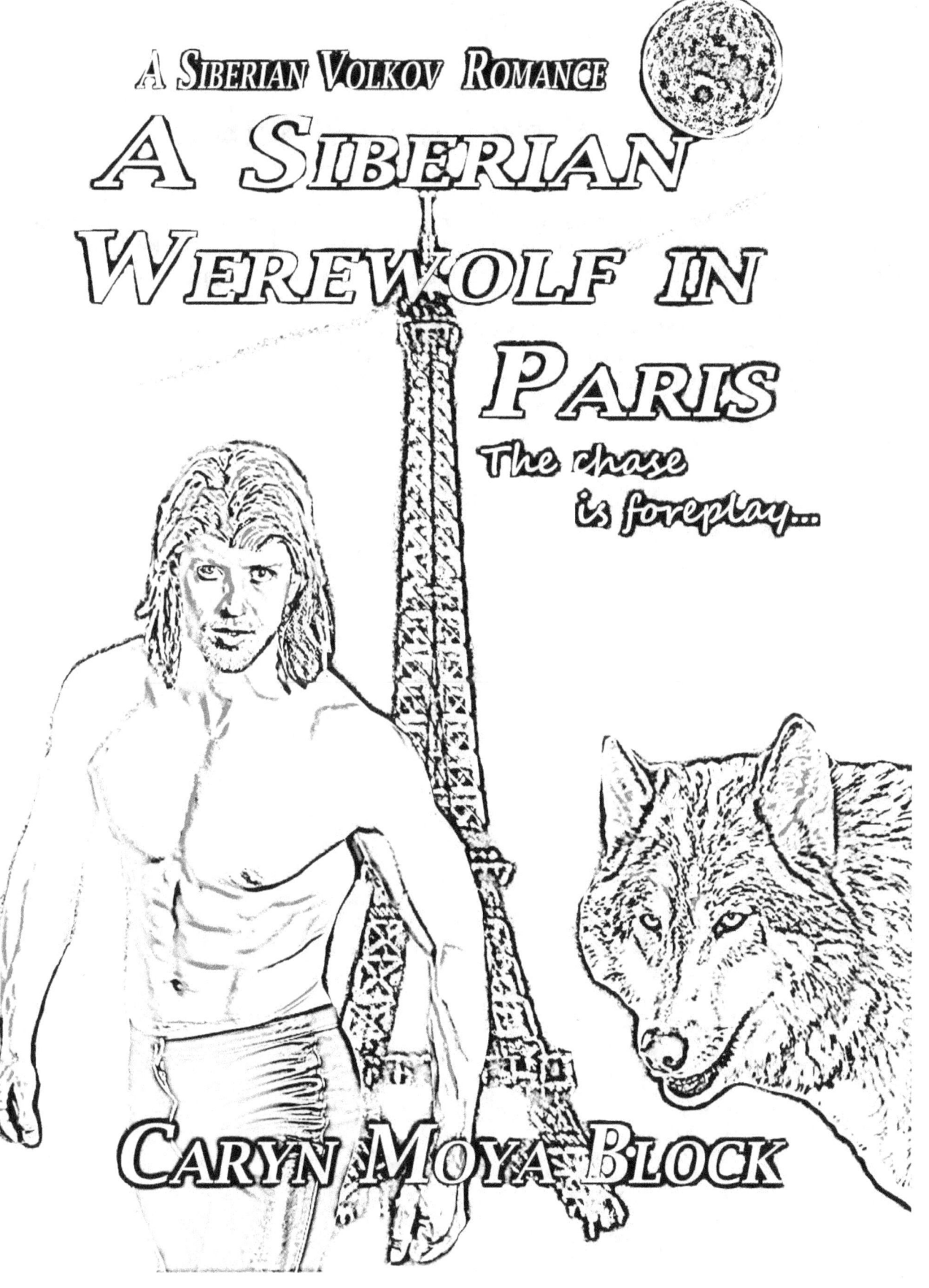

A SIBERIAN VOLKOV ROMANCE

A SIBERIAN WEREWOLF IN PARIS

The chase is foreplay...

CARYN MOYA BLOCK

A Siberian Werewolf Christmas
Book Six of the Siberian Volkov Pack Romance Series

Margaret Brady knows she must be out of her mind to go to Siberia for Christmas. But her intuition won't let her turn down the invitation of her best friend, Violet Volkov. When she meets the good looking Vyacheslav Putyatinov, she knows just what she wants for Christmas.

Vyacheslav "Slava" Putyatinov thinks any human woman coming to the Siberian Lycan village will be trouble. But one unmated could be a disaster. When he is put in charge of the American siren he finds trouble can lead to desire.

A Siberian Werewolf Christmas

A Siberian Volkov Romance

Caryn Moya Block

Wolfe's Mate
Book Seven of the Siberian Volkov Pack Romance Series

When her brother accidentally turns her into a lycan, Esme Fortescue struggles to find her balance. Now, while her brother desperately attempts to return her humanity, her lycan heartmate seduces her in her dreams.

Jared Wolfe has waited six months before claiming his mate due to the death of his parents and becoming the new Alpha of the Quebec Province. When Esme is in an accident and her brother disappears, Jared decides he can't wait to claim her any longer. But will Esme consent to leave Europe and can his newly changed mate handle the new Alpha?

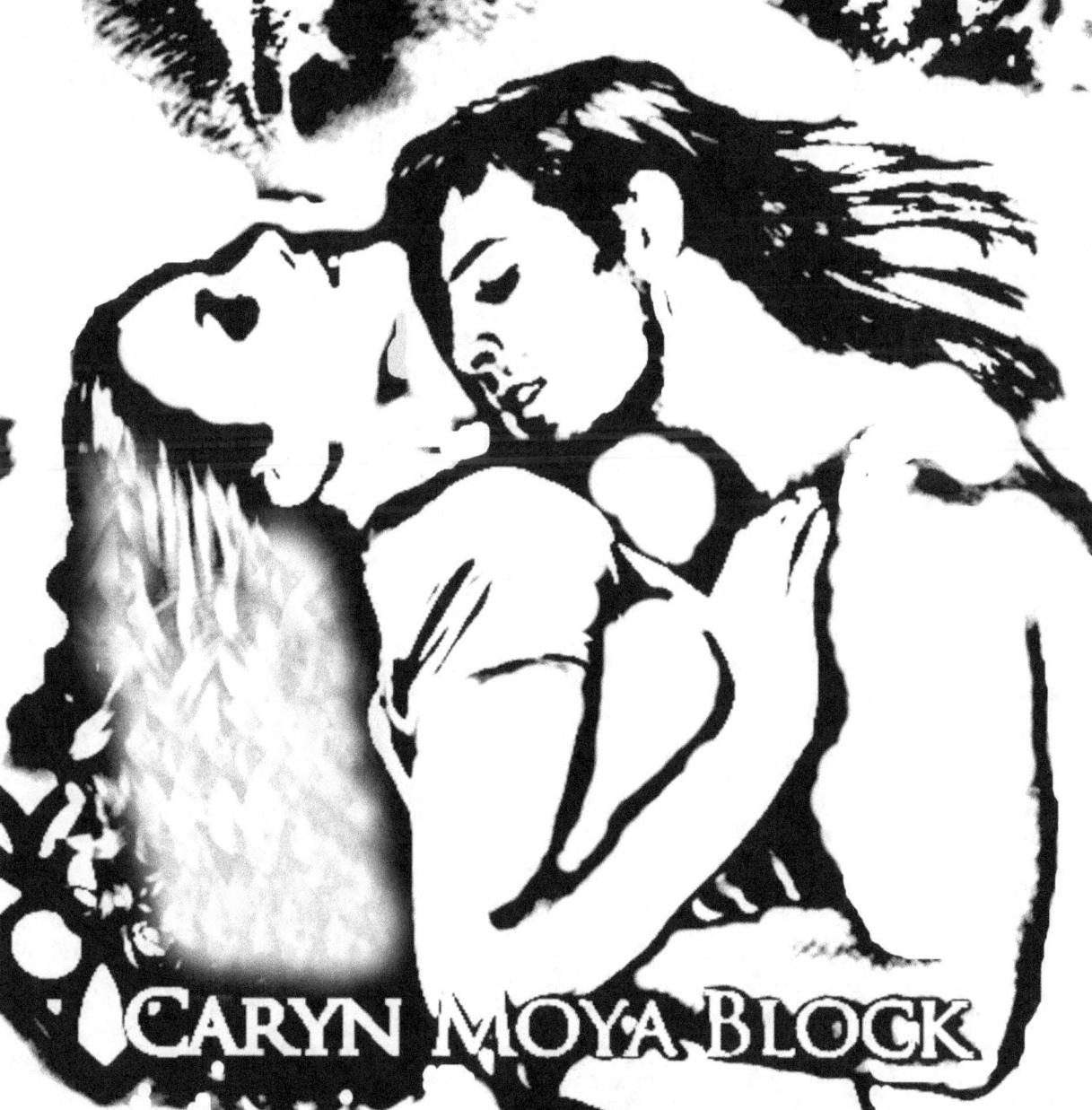

WOLFE'S MATE

CARYN MOYA BLOCK

Beta's Mate

Book Eight of the Siberian Volkov Pack Romance Series

Brenda Scott, while being cured of cancer, had her world turned upside down when she shifted into a wolf. Now living in Quebec with her new pack, she wonders if her dream of being in a special operations unit is forever out of reach. Then there is the quiet man who watches her with the yellow eyes of a wolf wanting his mate. Will she be able to adapt to her new wild urgings?

Granger Thibault wants his mate more than anything in the world. But he knows that if he pushes her, she will fight back. Once a soldier and the Alpha female's foster sister, Brenda is a force to be reckoned with. Can Granger find a way around Brenda's hard shell to the soft woman waiting to be loved?

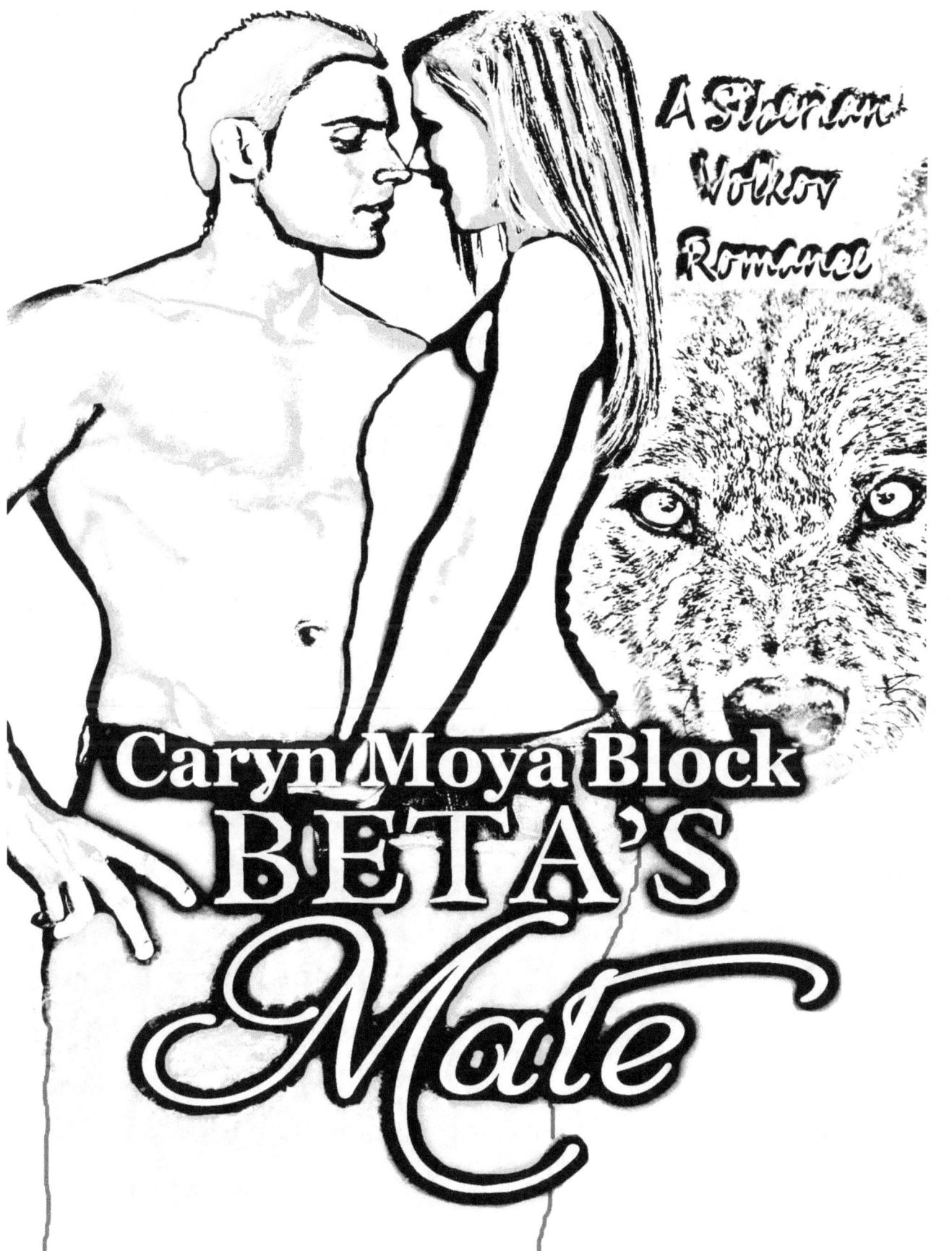

A Siberian
Volkov
Romance

Caryn Moya Block
BETA'S
Mate

The Gift of My Mate

Book Nine of the Siberian Volkov Pack Romance Series

Margot Martin has been searching for her mate for years. When she couldn't find a mate in her pack, she started looking for a mate in the human population, earning her a rather shady reputation. Now one of her human admirers has turned stalker and Margot can only turn to the head of pack security, Mathis Levesque, for help.

Mathis Levesque has known from the first moment he saw Margot Martin that she was his mate, a secret he has kept from her, for her own protection. A member of the Betas council's "Sable Guard" has made him more than one enemy and Mathis didn't want Margot to become a target. Now she is stalked by a human business man and Mathis must protect the one woman he can't give up.

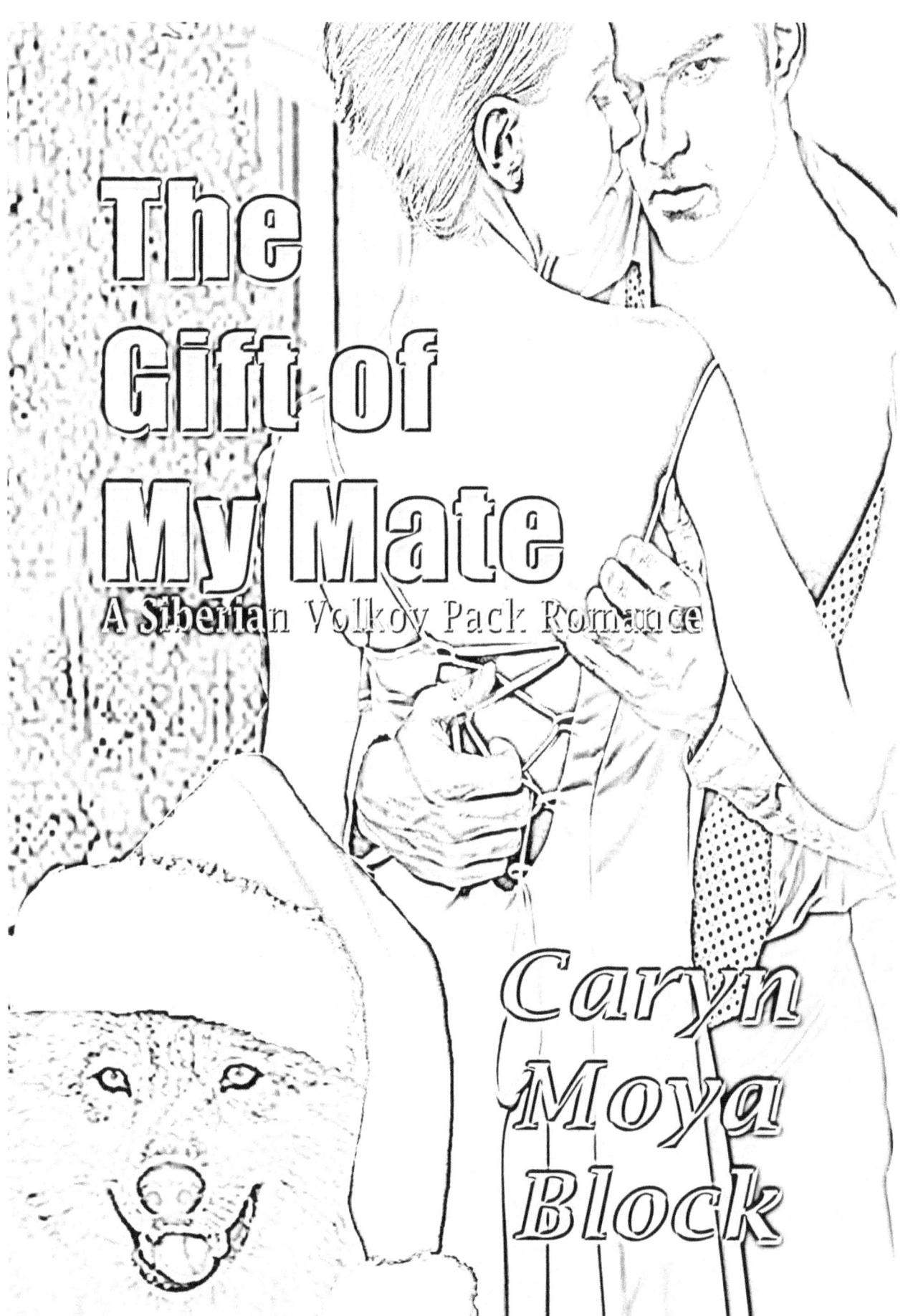

The Gift of My Mate

A Siberian Volkov Pack Romance

Caryn Moya Block

My Perfect Mate

Book Ten in the Siberian Volkov Pack Romance Series

Six months have passed since Susan Adams was forced to become a lycan. She's embraced the wolf with her whole heart, but having super senses and running on four feet can't help her keep a job or figure out where she belongs. Now, with a mating bond snapping into place and the mating heat riding her hard, Susan's wolf is demanding she cement the bond in place. There's only one problem. Her mate isn't a lycan. In fact, she's not sure what he is, and mating Susan is the farthest thing on his mind.

Jean Paul Nadeau is not your ordinary elemental witch. He's one of the famed Averys, as human witches know him. In truth, he is an immortal Fae Lord sent by the Queen of Avalon to guard a dimensional gateway sitting in the middle of Quebec City. When the lycan mating bond attaches to his heart, JP is both delighted and dismayed. Finding his "Destined One" is an unexpected gift, one that could cost him more than his immortality.

MY PERFECT MATE

Caryn Moya Block

Shadow Mate

Book Eleven in the Siberian Volkov Pack Romance Series

Sergei Sokolov, Siberian Lycan, is surprised when the mating bond snaps into place and connects him to a woman being attacked in Moscow. Knowing he may lose his destined mate sends him running to rescue her.

Lindy Quiet Thunder, Shadow Walker, is investigating strange lapses of lost time in a team of Marines. While taking the unit to Moscow for a little R&R, Lindy is attacked. As she loses consciousness her mind connects to her mate. Who is behind the attack and will her mate find her in time?

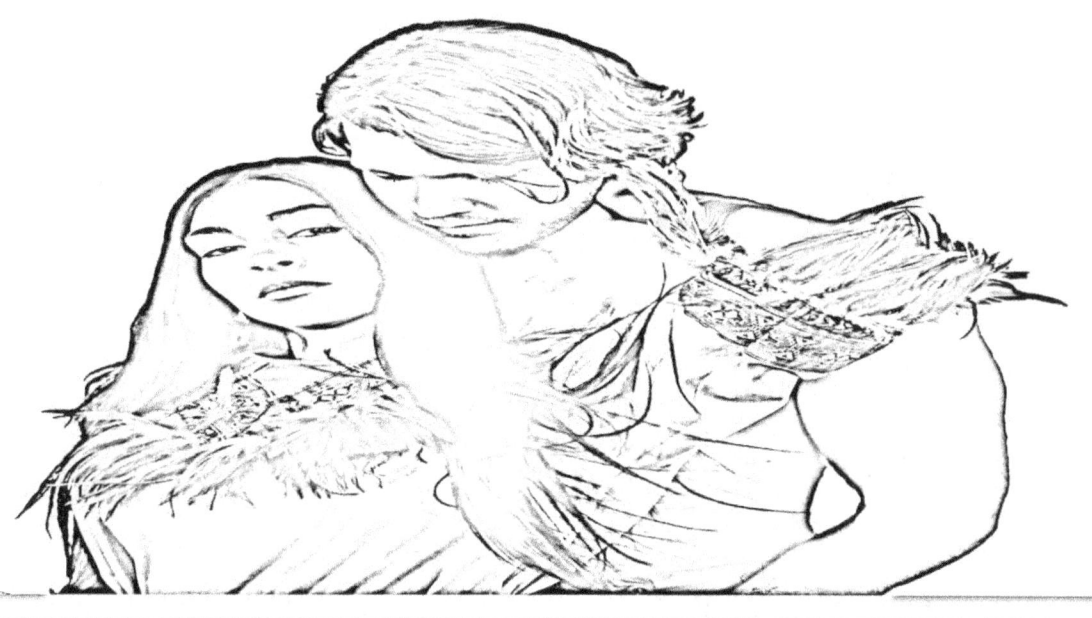

Shadow Mate

Shadow Walkers meet Siberian Lycans

Caryn Moya Block

Destined Magic

Book One of the Witch Guardian Romance Series
When Lycans and Witches meet.

Garrett Amhurst, a member of the Witch Guardian Police Force, investigates a claim of blood magic at the Blue Dolphin. He is surprised to find his "Destined One" is the owner. She isn't guilty of participating in the illegal rituals. But her sister is and it's Garrett's job to bring her to justice.

Gabriella Ross, Water Witch, knows her sister is hooked on the magic high of blood magic. But she can't turn her in to the Guardians. They would strip her sister of her magic. Gabriella would do anything to save her little sister, including stepping in front of a bullet.

DESTINED
MAGIC
A Witch Guardian Romance

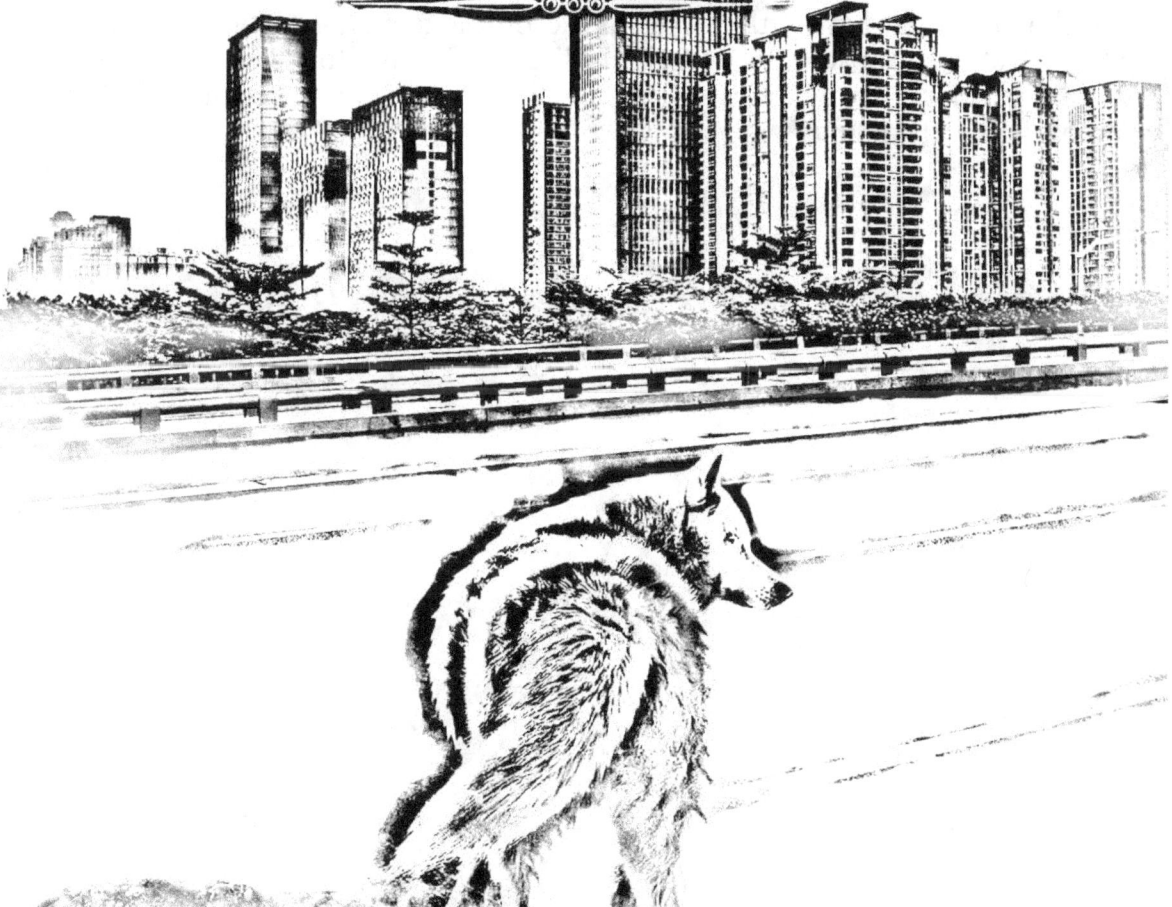

CARYN MOYA BLOCK

Aerial Magic

Book Two of the Witch Guardian Romance Series

Elise Delaire, the Guardian healer, goes to the bonding ceremony of her best friend. While there, Mabel Avery, the commander of the Guardians, introduces her to Curtis Brant. But when Elise shakes Brant's hand, she realizes that not only is this man not who he says he is, he is also her Destined One.

Owen Avery is on a mission from the queen of the Fae. Apprehend the rogue Fae who is now being called the Red Wizard. Everything is going according to plan until he shakes hands with the delectable Elise. Not only can she see through his disguise, but her touch causes his magic house tattoo to take on color, proving that she is his Destined One. Is he willing to give up his immortality and his home, the land of the Fae, to claim her?

Is love worth his immortality?

AERIAL MAGIC

A WITCH GUARDIAN ROMANCE

CARYN MOYA BLOCK

Fiery Magic

Book Three in the Witch Guardian Romance Series

Haytham Luften is an Air Witch Guardian supporting his team members while fighting Blood Cult members and the Marwolaeth possessed. He never expected to be gifted with a Destined One, or to hear his uncle, head of the Air House, threaten to renounce him if he dared claim the one woman who could share his magic.

Candace Kindle grew up on stories of "destined love" and sharing her magic with one special person. But with the Marwolaeth attacking, true love will have to wait for another day. Following her brother's advice she walks through a dimensional portal to take shelter with her mother and finds herself a slave in a land ruled by Dragons. There's only one person who can save her, the Destined One she walked away from.

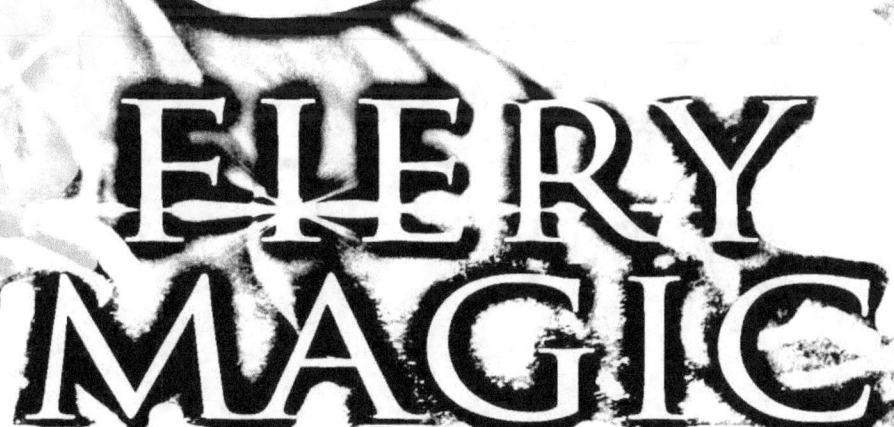

FIERY MAGIC

A WITCH GUARDIAN ROMANCE

CARYN MOYA BLOCK

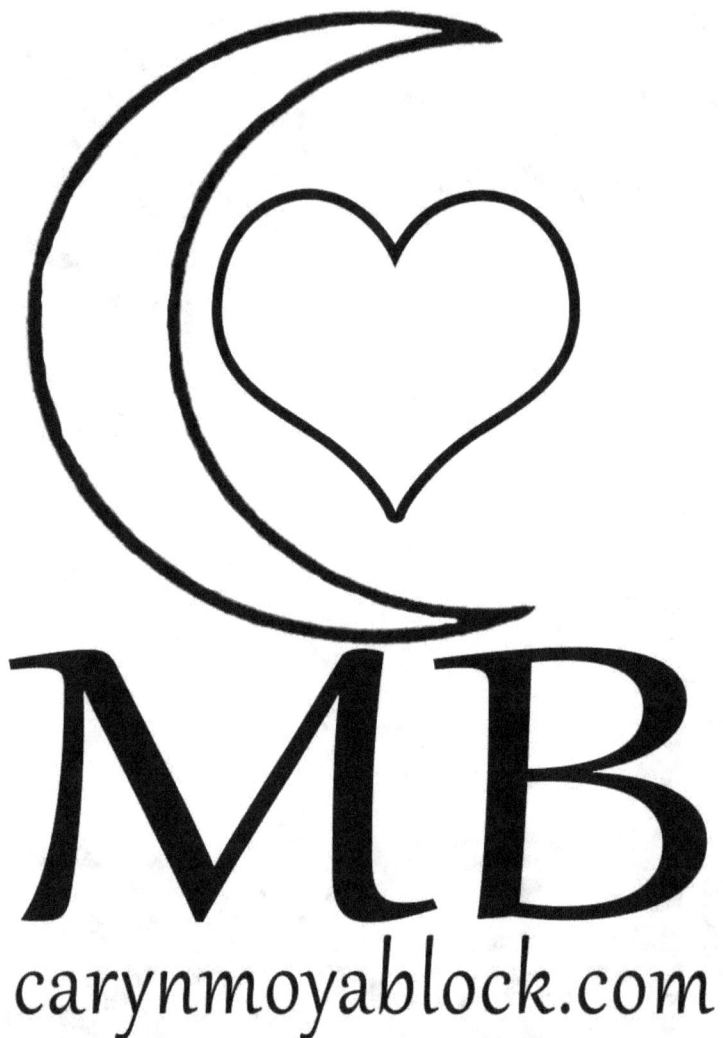

MB

carynmoyablock.com